Lollipops

Poetry and Prose

Andrew W. Lankford

Andrew W. Lankford
Lollipops

Andrew W. Lankford
Lollipops

Andrew W. Lankford
Lollipops

D W B   P U B L I S H I N G
www.dancingwithbearpublishing.com

Andrew W. Lankford
Lollipops

Andrew W. Lankford
Lollipops

for Jack, Paul, and Zoe
for showing me how better to live

Dear Reader

Thank you for choosing to take this journey with me. It means more than you'll ever know. I hope you realize that you are special and your potential great. And I hope that if nothing else, you will carry away a new longing and fascination for life. That's the gift we still have after all. Please know that you are loved. And though this moment may seem too difficult to get through, you are strong, and you will get through.

-Andrew

Andrew W. Lankford
Lollipops

Morning Prayer

Thanks for a good night's sleep
and for this quiet time where I
can lay bare my soul,
reflect on my life,
expel my deepest darkest secrets.
I don't know why You stay so close
when You could be anywhere
doing anything in the universe.
But You hear every word I say,
every breath I breathe,
even when I can't speak
or stop shivering.
Thanks for a good night's sleep
and for this quiet time now,
the love that You are,
the love You will always be.
Please take my heart
and do with it what You will.

Along the Coast

This is our place
where we can let go,
be ourselves,
let our minds break free
as long as we want,
as long as it takes,
as long as we need.
This is our place
along the coast
without rocks or sand or sea.

You Are You

It's alright
if you sit and gaze at the sky
and remember
the journey that has brought you here.
It's alright
if you laugh or you cry,
if you fear of never returning,
if you dream of going again.
You are you,
a dream come true
and always worth the fight.

You May Be

If you believe
you are an eagle soaring over trees,
knock yourself out,
who am I to tell you that you're not an eagle,
and what harm are you doing anyway?
Even if you are scaring a few people
by flapping your arms
and occasionally squawking,
you may be inspiring others
to reach inside themselves
and pull out the weights
that have held them down for so long.
You may be what someone is looking for.
You may be the only thing they ever see.

Maybe

Maybe
we suffer
so someone else
won't have to suffer
as much.
Maybe
things falling apart
around us
are actually coming together.
Maybe
what's truly going on
behind it all
is too much
for us to handle
alone.
Maybe
we were meant
for each other.
And maybe
just maybe
our purpose on this Earth is love.
If we knew for sure
would it make a difference?
Would we make a change?

A Beautiful Song

Take heart friends,
we're never alone,
but always a part of a beautiful song,
a song so compelling, so moving, so light,
it brings out the sunshine
and scatters the night.
Take heart friends,
it's not long
until we leave Earth
and fly to our home,
there to remain and forever belong,
much more than a part of a beautiful song,
having become that beautiful song.

We Should Listen

Though different,
the dusk and the dawn
are part of the same sun.
Without groaning or complaining,
and regardless of our understanding
or lack of appreciation,
they continue doing their jobs perfectly.
Before we lift another finger
against one another,
we should listen to them;
for they have much to say,
and though we think we know so much,
we have much left to learn.

Andrew W. Lankford
Lollipops

Waiting

Good things come to those who wait- Unknown

I've been told the best thing to do when worrying is to think about the worst thing that can happen. But standing there on my wedding day, in front of that crowd, waiting for my bride to walk down the aisle, thinking about the worst thing that could happen was not helping.

For the first couple of minutes I thought something might have gone wrong with her dress, a small tear perhaps that only needed a quick mend. That thought put me at ease. But as those first couple of minutes grew into more minutes, my face began to burn, and I couldn't keep my hands and knees from shaking. I believed she had changed her mind, packed her bags, climbed into a taxi, and was speeding toward the airport.

The church auditorium was as quiet as a cemetery at midnight, and looks of pity and concern showed on the faces of my family and friends, especially on the face of my mother on the front row. Beads of sweat rolled down my face and tension had its hands around my throat, squeezing.

Although I tried to stay calm, a tempest swirled in my mind. How would I explain this? How would I live the rest of my life with this rejection? Tension squeezed harder, unmercifully. Just as I was about give up and walk away, a phone rang in the foyer of the auditorium.

My father, who was the minister conducting the wedding, said loudly, "That is probably her, just calling to say she is running late."

Even though it wasn't her on the phone, the tension lifted slightly. A moment later, she appeared in the back of the auditorium, glowing like an angel, her smile brightening the room. Everyone stood while she walked down the aisle toward me. I wiped my face one more time before she reached me, but she knew I had been sweating.

She still takes tremendous delight in that.

If you're wondering why it took my wife so long to walk down the aisle during our wedding, it so happens it was a traditional Irish wedding, and the groom must wait on the bride. That's what is expected.

I love the rich symbolism of that tradition, but I wish I'd known about it beforehand. Life would've been much easier. However, without going through that tortuous waiting, this story would not exist, and besides, my wife was, and will always be, worth the wait.

Talking

A mother, father and their baby girl sat on the floor in the living room. The mother pointed to her shirt and said, "What color is my shirt?"

"Boo," the baby said.

"It's not blue," mother said. "It's white. Can you say white?"

"Boo," the baby giggled.

The father taps his feet together and said, "What color are my socks?"

"Boo," the baby said.

"They're not blue," the father said. "They're black. Can you say black?"

"Boo," the baby said, eyes shining.

The mother, father, and their baby girl sit on the floor in the living room and talk late into the evening. They are not aware of the radiance spreading from their windows, spreading into the sky, helping many people find their way home, causing Satan to shiver slightly, then shade his eyes.

A Good Moment

While unloading dishes from the dishwasher,
my daughter scooted close to me. I picked her
up and sat her on the edge of the sink. I took
out a fork, held it close to her and turned it
quickly.

Sunlight came through the window,
caught the fork just right and made it sparkle.
Her eyes grew large and she babbled something.
I wondered what was going through her mind.

Probably best not knowing. I do know she was
lovely watching me unload the rest of the dishes,
looking more like her mother and less like me.

Behind the Shower Curtain

My daughter had been too quiet
for too long in the back of the house,
so I went to check on her.
She heard me coming
and was already hiding
behind the shower curtain when I got there.
Her feet were showing
under the curtain like two shy animals.
She had been playing in the nail polish again,
and spilled a bottle of the stuff on the floor.
As I cleaned, I called out her name,
making her believe I didn't know she was there.
After cleaning the mess,
I gently pulled back the shower curtain
and saw her looking out the other side for me.
That's the way I must appear to God
after doing things I know better than doing,
hiding behind my shower curtain,
my two feet showing,
looking for Him out one side
as He looks at me tenderly from the other.

For My Daughter

One morning
when you were two years old,
you came over,
put your little hand on my arm,
and gave me a kiss on the cheek.
I thought about the significance
of what you'd done
and how much it meant to me,
but I couldn't find the words.
The more I thought,
the more expressionless I became.
I wanted to write something
about that moment,
but I couldn't do it at the time.
For now, my daughter,
I put my little hand on your arm,
give you a kiss on the cheek
and say once again that I love you.
Wherever you go
in this crazy world,
you are never alone.
I hope these simple words
will help you think clearly
when it's time for you
to stand up and speak.

Andrew W. Lankford
Lollipops

Blowing on a Fly

My boys take great pleasure
in blowing on a fly
as we eat pancakes in the kitchen.

There's nothing I could do or say
that would be as funny to them
as it is to blow on the fly,
watch it circle away,
come back and land
in puddles of syrup.

The fly is a true entertainer,
a tiny Charlie Chaplain with wings,
silent, yet deliciously jolly.

Together at the Dinner Table

Many things spilled
at our dinner table
over the years.
One particular evening,
pasta sauce splattered
all over the floor and walls
and even went into your hair.
When we had ice cream later,
it dribbled down the cones,
down our chins,
and onto your brand new clothes.
I want you to know
I'm far from perfect,
but today when I felt
I had everything sorted out,
I spilled coffee on my new shoes,
and when I kneeled to clean them,
the more I cleaned,
the deeper the stain became.
I am far from perfect
and never too old to learn a thing or two.
I suppose as long as we live,
no matter how far we may drift apart,
we will always be together at the dinner table,
making a nasty mess,
depending on Someone much greater
to help us clean up our lives.

Questions on a Tuesday Night

Daddy, what do our souls look like?
Will we feel anything when our souls leave our bodies?
Where will our souls go?
How long will it take our souls to get there?
Will we know anything after we die?
Daddy, what will Heaven be like?
Will it be boring?
Can we play?
Can I ask Jesus questions?
Will Jesus ever get tired of talking with me?
How much longer until we get to Heaven?
Why can't we go on now?
Daddy, how much longer is this going to take?

Understanding a Little More

For years,
I've spent evenings
with my children
sharing great moments
from the movie, *Star Wars*.
I've even gone so far
as to tell them that I'm a Jedi
and that as a youngster
I fought many galactic battles
side-by-side with Luke Skywalker and Yoda.
They believe what I tell them,
even that I have a light-saber
locked away just in case
Darth Vader attacks our house.
The other day,
my wife was rushing
to make a doctor's appointment,
and I was helping her load the children into the van,
making sure they were buckled safely in their seats.
In the midst of the rush
my children began saying
how much they love the movie, *Star Wars*.
As I buckled my daughter,
I told them I loved the movie too.
One of my boys looked at me seriously and said,
"But daddy, you are *Star Wars*."
I closed the side doors of the van
and watched my wife drive away,
understanding a little more
how much it truly means to be here.

Andrew W. Lankford
Lollipops

The Toy Robot

If I've told my children once,
I've told them a thousand times
to keep the toys with batteries inside the house.
But I might as well be talking to the mailbox.

Out on the porch the other morning,
enjoying a nice cup of coffee,
I heard one of their toy robots
speaking from behind the bushes.

Because of the rain the night before,
its voice was slow and shaky,
saying over and over, "Stop or I'll shoot."

Although this will never be recorded
in the annals of world history,
it was a pivotal point in my life,
one of the few times I had been right.

After drinking my coffee,
I brought my children outside
to see their expressions when they saw
the sad condition of their toy robot.

I expected a pat on the back,
expected them to tell me how brilliant I was,
but all they did was laugh and scamper back
into the house to watch cartoons.

Andrew W. Lankford
Lollipops

The next morning I was out again
having a cup of coffee.
The toy robot was in the middle of the yard,
among other toys with batteries,

not even trying to speak,
a haunting reminder
that though I had been right,
my children had not listened.

All It Takes

All it takes
for the children
to have a good time
is to chase each other
around a tree on their bicycles.

It was the same for me,
until I craved more.

Can I ever get back
on my bicycle
and chase my friends
around a tree?

All it takes
is more than I have.

The simple things
are no longer so simple.

On the Porch

Long before my family wakes up,
I sit on the porch and listen to the rain.

My thoughts are with me,
and like friends, take my hand,
and lead me back
to the coast of Northern Ireland,
where I spent so much time
looking at the sea
in cold driving wind,
wondering if God was hearing me.

The rain stops
and one of my boys
comes out on the porch
and says he's hungry.

Sure enough, God heard.

The Thunder Makers

*I*nside the house the children were frightened by the sound of thunder. Their father sat beside them and told them about the thunder makers. He explained that high above the clouds, thousands of horses played in a lush meadow, and when all those horses became hungry, they ran toward a magnificent fruit tree. He went on to explain the sound of thunder was only the sound of those pretty horses running through the meadow. The children relaxed.

The story of the thunder makers stuck with them through the years. And as more storms came, they asked more detailed questions about the horses, the meadow and the fruit tree. Their father absolutely loved making up answers to their questions, so much so that he wished there were more storms so he could spend more time with his children.

Years passed and the children moved away. Their father missed them dearly, but he understood. One day, a great storm blew in, and thunder rumbled and shook the house, and he went outside for a closer look. When he looked up, he saw clouds in the shape of horses moving gracefully through the sky. He couldn't take his eyes away from them. As more thunder roared, he remembered the first time he sat down and helped his little ones through the storm. He felt both happy and sad, but more than anything, he felt mighty blessed to have been a part of such a wonderful thing.

Later, after the storm passed, he wanted to call his children and tell them about the storm and the horses he'd seen in the clouds, but he knew wherever his children were in the world, they had seen them too.

Andrew W. Lankford
Lollipops

Meeting Jealousy

No matter if it was raining or snowing, Ms. Gillespie was always the first person in the village walking along the riverside. That was the thing she could always brag about and it meant the world to her. There came a time, however, as usually does, when another person grew jealous of hearing from the villagers how Ms. Gillespie was always the first.

One morning, a younger woman decided to take action. She woke up early and ran as fast as she could to the riverside. When she got there, she discovered she had beaten Ms. Gillespie, and felt very proud of herself. But since it was so early, no one was there to witness her accomplishment. The only thing she could think to do was sit and wait until Ms. Gillespie arrived, and then jump up and proclaim her victory. She had it all figured out.

As the stars disappeared and the sun began lighting the sky, a figure approached her. This figure was wearing a long robe and hood and walked with a limp. "I say," the young woman said, "nice morning isn't it?"

The figure slowly removed the hood from its face. Lightning blazed where eyes should've been. As you can imagine, the young woman was terrified and began trembling and wanted to run away, but she was frozen.

"I understand," the figure said in a booming voice, "that you have come to meet me."

The young woman replied, "No, not at all. I've come to beat Ms. Gillespie to the riverside."

The figure bowed its head as if in prayer, as if gaining strength, and looked again at the young woman. Lightning blazed more savagely. Enjoying the moment, it said, "You've come to meet me then."

The young woman could barely breathe. A few minutes later, Ms. Gillespie found the young woman sitting alone, shaking violently and mumbling to someone only she could see. Ms. Gillespie put her arm around the young woman and held her for a very long time. Then she helped her stand and walk home. From then on, Ms. Gillespie and the young woman were the first two people walking along the riverside every morning.

Andrew W. Lankford
Lollipops

Breaking the Rules

He was a good man, standing beside a pond in his old boots, tossing bread to the ducks near a sign that said, "Don't feed the ducks."

But a thousand men couldn't have stopped him because he loved the ducks and knew them as intimately as he knew his own children. He spoke to them as he tossed more bread, and then noticed a nest with eggs. But this nest, he knew, was sitting too far out in the open, a very dangerous place. So he moved the nest and saw that some of the eggs were already hatched. It nearly broke his heart.

Later, he wasn't there when the other eggs hatched, when those tiny eyes opened, when those tiny bodies wavered in the wind. The good man in his old boots was never there again. But someone else stepped in to take his place, to continue feeding the ducks near a sign that said, "Don't feed the ducks."

Strange Things Are Happening

Ms. McGee was the type of person people went to with their problems. She made time to listen and tried to make things better. She spent much of her time in the lobby of the retirement home, comforting, encouraging, even laughing and crying with others.

One night, the lobby was packed and everyone was having a good time, swapping gossip and stories from the past. Then, for apparently no reason at all, Ms. McGee got up from the sofa, went over to the young security guard sitting behind his desk and said with a little smirk, "Son, strange things are happening."

The security guard nodded his head and said, "I think you're right." That's what he always said when a resident told him something. It was just the easiest way to go.

After a few minutes, Ms. McGee came back to him and said, "Strange things are happening."

Again he nodded and said, "I think you're right." After a few more minutes, and after third time of her telling him the same thing over again, the young security guard began believing she might have a drop or two of the crazy blood.

As the evening went on, what she said perplexed him deeply and drew him further into thought. When the residents began leaving the lobby for the night, he got up from his desk and walked over to Ms. McGee.

"Ms. McGee," he said, "when you say strange things are happening, what do you mean?"

Stunned, her eyes grew wet, her countenance fell, and it seemed her spirit had left her body. She put her head down and walked toward the elevator. He had struck a nerve, tapped into her secret, the delicate thing that made her who she was. He badly wanted her to come back and answer his question, but he had the decency to let her go. He walked back to his desk, realizing there are things in life better not knowing.

Searching

The deli-man busily sliced ham behind the counter of the grocery store. News spread that Mrs. Sims, the district manager, was coming that afternoon for a visit. The buzz of this news spread around the store, but the deli-man wasn't overly concerned about the promise of this visit. He was content with his station in life. He had gorgeous children, a gorgeous wife, and a nice house to live in. His job supplied everything his family needed.

But when Mrs. Sims arrived that afternoon, he rushed to one of the shelves on the sales floor and began straightening cans that didn't need straightening. His heart beat rapidly as Mrs. Sims approached, and he began rehearsing what he might say if she spoke to him. But she passed by without saying a word. Disheartened, he went back behind the counter and started slicing ham again.

What he didn't realize, was that Mrs. Sims was also searching for someone to speak to her, searching for someone right in front of her eyes.

Living the Dream

Although he baked the best loaves of bread in town, he was more than a baker. When customers came into his bakery, he took the time to listen to what they had to say, for as long as it took.

One morning, as he was placing some fresh loaves on the rack above the counter, a woman came into the bakery. She looked sad and her hair was tangled and undone. She had bags around her eyes, and her dress was wrinkled and worn. When he asked her how she was doing, immediately, she told him how for many years she had dreamed of becoming a singer.

She went on to say that she had several kids, and when she wasn't taking care of them she worked long hours at a fast-food restaurant, and that by the time she got home, she was too exhausted to work on her music.

The baker felt sorry for her, and told her to never give up on her dream. Then he astonished her by asking her to sing for him. He sat at one of the small tables and she closed her eyes and began to sing.

During her song, he thought back to the time he had dreamed of being a famous artist, traveling around the world, having his name in lights. After she finished her song, she thanked him for listening. He told her it was his pleasure and that she had a wonderful voice.

She left the bakery, and he went into the backroom and began mixing dough. But she was still there with him, as were all the customers he'd helped through the years. There in the backroom of the bakery he was the artist he'd always dreamed of being. There, he was living the dream.

Parts

An old man reads a sign
in front of a church building:
"Which part of you belongs to God?"

Having lost his teeth a few years ago,
he thinks about those words,
and he walks away wondering
is it possible his teeth are now with God.

He thinks there may be a chance
his teeth are on display
in a shabby cabin deep in the woods,
a place angels can go when needing a break
from all that glitter and gold.

Before reaching home,
he walks by an old woman without eyebrows.
He chuckles. She looks at him hatefully.
But when he smiles, she opens up
and laughs as freely as a waterfall.

Getting Much Too Close

A young teacher
gave her students an assignment
from the workbook.
Then she began walking around the room
to make sure they understood.
She glanced over the shoulder
of a boy drawing a picture
of a dragon breathing fire into a village.
Her eyes met his eyes.
She told him to put away the drawing
and start working on the assignment.
However, when she came back,
he was still drawing,
and she noticed
that he'd drawn
big tears raining from the eyes of the dragon.
Her eyes met his eyes.
But curious as to what he would draw next,
she moved on quietly to help other students.
When she returned,
the drawing was gone
and the boy was working on the assignment.
Her eyes never met his eyes again.

Lollipops

I know I should not do this,
a terrible breach of teaching etiquette
that may land me in teacher purgatory,
but I'm going to share a secret
shared to me by an old teacher
a few days before her retirement.
She told me that when students get crazy,
really out of control,
to go over to my desk
without saying a word
and take a few lollipops out of the drawer.
Well, the day came
when my students went totally bonkers
and I pulled a few lollipops out of the drawer.
Calm swept through the room,
and intelligent questions began being asked
by students I'd thought were from distant planets.
I thought the end of the world was near,
that soon I'd hear the blast of trumpets,
see legions of angels plunge from the sky.
Lollipops had taken those students
to a place I could never take them to.
I popped a lollipop in my mouth
and gladly joined them there.

An Ode to the Lollipop

Before this year,
I never thought much of you,
just popped you in my mouth
and went on my way.
But through the course of this school year,
I've come to appreciate your amazing power,
and you've become more than a lollipop to me.
To call you an angel might be pushing it,
but it's not too far off the mark.
I'm sorry I didn't rely on you sooner,
that I believed I could do everything myself.
But you were patient
and like the father with his prodigal son,
you welcomed me with open arms.
I will forever be thankful to you.
You are my knight in shining armor.
May you live on to instruct
and inspire students until the end of time.

Andrew W. Lankford
Lollipops
When She Stepped Outside

On a Friday afternoon,
after a hectic week,
Mrs. Crystal made a deal
with her seventh-grade students.
She told them that if they were quiet
and listened to a short story
she'd take them outside
for the rest of the day.

She pushed play on the recording
and cut off the lights and her students
went silent as graves,
even those students who despised her
and wanted nothing more
than to shove her off a cliff
then drag her body through the city streets.

Mrs. Crystal leaned back in her chair
and threw her legs on the desk.
She went to her favorite place,
the place she went to at times like this.

When the recording stopped,
she sighed, forced herself up,
and waited as the students ran out of the room.
She shut and locked the door
and followed them down the hallway.

And when she stepped outside
and watched her students play,
she was still able to think clearly
and appreciate
those happy young lives she held in her hands.

Awfully Glad

While I was teaching from behind the podium, one student was making a paper airplane, one student was popping chewing gum like crazy, while another crawled around the room like a zombie. But no matter how much they tried to get on my nerves, they couldn't knock the good feeling out of me.

As a teacher I'm supposed to want what's best for them, and I felt bad they were failing so miserably, and a few times I wanted them to succeed, but I kept my head on straight and didn't let up.

For one of the few times in my teaching career, I kept my good feeling until the day was over. Don't ask me how I did it. I don't know.

And I'm awfully glad I don't know, because I couldn't handle the media attention, the guest appearances on the late night shows, the paparazzi following me everywhere, all those lucrative book deals.

Andrew W. Lankford
Lollipops

Teaching

My students aren't looking in books;
they're too busy looking at me for answers.
Though flattering, it's daunting
having students looking at me all the time.

I want to slam my fist on the desk
and tell them to stop looking at me,
that I don't know everything,
that I'm made from the same stuff
they are.

But fear holds me back
like it's always held me back,
and will continue holding me back
until I put my foot down
and meet it face-to-face.

I am certain there will come a time
when I'll leave the classroom
to become the person I was before.
By then I hope and pray my students
will know better than to follow.

Trembling

She stands from her desk
and moves around the room
like a phantom with nowhere to go.

She speaks to her students,
not caring her breath smells of stale coffee.

The students hear her voice,
but they know she is not there.

They tell her things that would make
a normal person tremble.

She takes those things
home with her that night
and locks them away
with a trembling hand.

Andrew W. Lankford
Lollipops

Paper Airplanes

$\mathscr{I}$ had many nightmares as a teacher, but this one in particular struck my fancy. The students had me tied me to a chair and were slapping me until I caved in to their demands and gave them extra credit on their exams.

Then they released me from the chair, having me thinking things were back to normal. And then, just as I was getting my confidence back, they started hurling paper airplanes at my head. These paper airplanes flew clean through my head and, as if glazed by my brain, came out of my head all silvery and shiny.

I don't claim to be an interpreter of dreams, not even close, but there must be something to this dream, some hidden meaning or significance. The one thing I liked was that the paper airplanes came out of my head silvery and shiny. That's a good thing, isn't it?

It could've been worse. They could've come out of my head all dark and gooey. So what I'll do is this—I'll ignore all the psychiatry and wise philosophy, and I'll say the dream means I have a bright, intelligent, transforming kind of mind.

Hey, if I don't say it no one else will. And besides, what's the harm in having a little fun every once in a while, especially if most of the fun usually comes at my expense?

Andrew W. Lankford
Lollipops

Homework

Even if you didn't hear
a single word I said,
I listened closely to you.
You see,
this learning thing
is a two-way street,
far beyond the reach of books,
windows of classrooms,
hallways of schools.
For homework,
translate this Latin phrase:
Omnia vincit amor.
Keep it in your heart
as far as you go.
You will be quizzed later;
you can count on that.

Andrew W. Lankford
Lollipops

Love Has A Way

Even as hatred
is performing on stage,
love has a way
of working
her magic.

The Bird's Song

A boy was alone, playing in the woods far from his home. He kicked rocks, threw sticks, splashed around in the creek, having the time of his life, and suddenly he lost his sight. He tripped and fell and he tried to see, but the more he tried, the scarier things became.

A red bird flying close by, singing wildly, and heard the boy crying. It stopped singing and flew down to the boy's shoulder. Like a child first learning how to pray, it closed its eyes and began singing like it had never sung before. The song passed from the bird into the boy, and the boy could see again.

The boy jumped up and ran for home, never looking back at the bird, not understanding the price that had been paid for him to see again. Having lost its song, the red bird flew silently, yet more joyfully than ever; for the boy's sight had now become the bird's song.

The Lonely Rose

There lived a rose on a rosebush that had no scent. As you might imagine, the rose grew very lonely and sad. One day, the rose decided to speak out and try to make things better. A bumblebee flew close and the rose said, "Mr. Bumblebee, do you know why I don't smell like the other roses here?"

The bumblebee hovered in the air and scratched its head. "I don't have time for such useless questions. I'm hungry and I need some honey." That answer upset the rose.

Later on, an ant crawled close and the rose said, "Mr. Ant, do you know why I don't smell like the other roses here?"

The ant thought for a moment then said, "Must be something wrong with you. Yes that's it. Something is dreadfully wrong with you." The ant crawled away in line with the other ants. That answer made the rose cry and cry.

In the middle of all that crying, a bird landed close by. "What's wrong with you my friend?"

The rose looked at the bird and said, "I don't smell like the other roses here, and I feel lonely."

"If you think that's bad," the bird said, "try flying through the sky without being able to sing."

This astonished the rose. "What do you mean?"

"Some time ago," the bird said, "I gave up my song to help a boy see again. But it's been the best thing I've ever done, because I get to fly over and watch him grow and be happy, and that makes me happy."

From then on, the bird and the rose became best friends and helped each other. They spent many wonderful hours together, and sometimes they laughed so loudly, you'd think they hadn't a care in the world.

Andrew W. Lankford
Lollipops

Laughter

$\mathcal{A}$ man had many worries and went outside, trying to get those worries off his mind. While standing in his yard, he began to hear laughter. Laughter so free and happy and infectious, he wanted to be able to laugh like that.

He went back inside his house and tried to laugh the way he'd heard, but his laughter was cold and forced and mechanical, and the more he tried, the worse it became. He went back outside to find who had been laughing, and whether or not they would teach him.

He discovered the laughter came from a rosebush on the side of his house, and when he stepped close, he saw a bird next to a rose.

"I hate to disturb you," the man said, "but can you tell me how you laugh like that?"

The bird said, "You don't know me, but I certainly know you. You remember the day you were in the woods playing and you lost your sight? I was the one who gave up my song to restore your sight."

The man stood there, thinking back to that day he remembered so well. "You gave up your song for me?" he asked.

"Oh yes my friend," the bird said, "and it was the best decision I ever made. I've been taking great delight in your joy ever since."

Then the rose said, "And there came a day when I felt really bad because I didn't smell like the other roses on this bush, but my friend here came along and helped me. Since that time, we've helped many others get through their struggles. That's why we can laugh like we do, because we love others, and we love life."

The man knelt down and thanked the bird and the rose for their kindness. "Oh enough of this," the bird said, "join us. Let go, and think about all the blessings you have."

And that's just what happened. The three of them began laughing so beautifully that birds came from all over the world over to hear them. And from that moment on, the man's life changed for the better, and he went out of his way to help others.

He never had trouble laughing again.

The Red Bird

The red bird
picked at a crumb
on the ground.
It looked around
and met my eyes.
I think I saw
someone I knew.
It flew away
and left me hoping
for life after death,
left me wishing
I could peek behind the veil
between here and there,
left me feeling
and reaching for words.

Love Is So Cool

Love is so cool on her throne,
her long robe
and long silver hair
blowing in the wind,
her breathtaking eyes
not needing a thing.
Love is so cool on her throne,
grooving to her own beat,
doing her own thing.
Her voice,
full of strains of many songs,
persuades even devils
to fling open their windows
and hum along.

Knowing My Luck

Some people believe
angels and demons
always surround us,
fighting for control of our souls.
If that's the case,
it would explain
all those strange groaning noises
I heard in my kitchen this morning
as I was scrambling eggs.
Now I'm driving to work,
I don't see how these angels and demons
have managed to squeeze inside my car.
They must be terribly cramped,
unless they can use their superpowers
and shrink to the size of bedbugs.
I guess it's possible.

As I merge into traffic
I imagine these tiny angels and demons
flipping around the dashboard
like incredible acrobats,
swinging swords and axes
as if the world might end any moment
and my eternal fate with it.

Andrew W. Lankford
Lollipops

Thinking all this is happening,
it would be easy freaking out
and losing control of the car,
but a good song has come on the radio,
a soft song that puts the mind at ease.
I crank up the volume.

Knowing my luck,
these angels and demons will get so upset
by me enjoying myself for once,
they'll clasp hands
and swear allegiance to each other.
But all I can do for now
is concentrate on this heavy traffic,
keep my eyes open and sing along.

Heartburn

I'm tossing and turning and trying to sleep,
but this burning in my chest will not go away.

When I was younger I would've said this pain
was being caused by my soul trying to find a
way out of my body. Now I know that's not it
at all; it's simply stomach acid working its way
back up that's causing this burning, simple as
that. Lucky for me, the drug store is still open,

I have money and a quick way to get there,
and my soul seems satisfied being where it is.

Stuck Imagining

Taking a bottle
of heartburn tablets from the shelf,
I find a small ceramic figurine on the floor.
It has wings and looks so sad and delicate,
I have to pick it up
and hold it to my chest.
On the way out of the drug store,
I take the figurine to the cashier,
thinking she'll keep it and find the owner,
but when I hand it to her,
her eyes narrow,
and wicked spreads across her face.
She throws it into the trash,
and it breaks into pieces.

I drive home
with an urge to go back
and tell the cashier how I feel.
But with the way my life is going,
she'd probably throw me in the trash
and break me into pieces.

Since my health insurance
would never cover those injuries,
I'm stuck imagining
the figurine piecing itself back together,
climbing out of the trash can,
and slapping the cashier across the face.
It may not be as good as the real thing,
but it sure beats letting her get away with it.

Andrew W. Lankford
Lollipops

Grasping For More

Driving home,
I see something
in the middle of the road.
I flash the high-beams.
It looks up;
its eyes flash unearthly blue.
Even through the high-beams,
it looks clear through me,
searching for something
I must not have.
It darts away,
leaving me
grasping for more.

Matching Socks

Doing laundry is as exciting to me
as I'm sure it is to you,
though I don't mind pulling
the big towels out of the pile;
kind of feels good watching
the pile topple over.

It's the socks that drive me bananas;
I can never find a matching pair.
What's worse is those odd socks
seemed please by me crawling
on my hands and knees
on the brink of exhaustion.

They must have a nervous tick
in their impish little minds
to want to see me suffer like that.
If I had treated them badly I'd understand.
But I've always worn them gently,
washed them in cool sudsy water,
and dried them with the softest air.
If anything, they should be thankful.

I've thought about calling my lawyer
and slapping a lawsuit on them.
But they'd just plead insanity
and end up on the feet of happy people
who care less if their socks match or not.

Andrew W. Lankford
Lollipops

Then I'd be left with no socks,
which would be a problem in this February chill.

I'll go on like I've been going,
pretending it doesn't matter as much as it does.
And maybe one day they'll get the hint
and make it easy for me to match them properly,
though the chances of that happening
are about as great as my feet
sprouting wings overnight.

Mowing the Yard

I'm mowing the yard
and things are going well
until I start thinking.
That's when the trouble begins.
I start thinking I should take more care
about what I'm wearing
the next time I'm mowing the yard,
that this tight tee-shirt
and bright Bermuda shorts
are doing me no favors with the neighbors.
Then I start thinking
I should stop thinking
and focus more on mowing the yard,
but that's about as possible
as cutting the rest of this grass
with a snap of the fingers.
If anything, I've learned
not to fight these thoughts too much,
but allow them to go wherever they need to go.
It's much easier that way,
and anyway, by not fighting as much,
I'll mow the yard faster,
and get inside to that glass of iced tea
that's never once thought badly of me.

Andrew W. Lankford
Lollipops

The Wasp

The wasp is here again
in the shade of my backyard.
It is such a dangerous thing,
but I must seem a dangerous thing to it too.
Why does it fly so close?
It could certainly sting me,
but I don't believe it will;
we share too much
this need to live another day.

All I See Is Me

When I look out the window all I see is me.
I do what I can, rub my eyes,
splash cold water on my face,
try to reason myself out of it,
but when I look again, all I see is me.
It is frightening seeing me
instead of trees and sky
and the other things that are out there.
How much will it cost to let myself go?
How painful can it really be?
I shut my eyes and close the blinds and walk away.
Tomorrow is another day
and I will try again
to find the trees and sky
and the other things that are out there.
I know they are waiting for me
and will continue waiting as long as it takes.

Going Back

I keep going back,
expecting different results,
but I always end up
with the same old thing,
the same disappointments,
the same bitter sting.
It would be nice,
just this once,
to keep going instead of going back,
but I fear if I cross that bridge
I will not be allowed to return.
Home is too dear,
that part of myself I can never be without.

Searching For A Way Out

Bad thoughts
are clawing at me again,
trying their hardest
to make me forget
that things
are as clear
as mist moving
beneath a waterfall.
But you know,
let those bad thoughts
claw all they want,
let them draw blood even;
I'm not giving up,
and I'm not about to forget
the good things in life,
the incredible kindness of strangers,
the angelic qualities of so many others.
This is my life,
the only one I'll ever have,
too good for anything but the best.

Doing

Knowing
what I had to do
never took me very far.
Doing
was the melody
that made my dark a star.

Revision

I would love this once to let go,
spread my wings,
let the flood gates open,
let the subconscious take over
and write down everything that's on my mind.
I'm sure this paper would receive it kindly,
wouldn't utter a word of protest.
But the filter of revision won't allow such things.
I suppose that's a good thing,
since what I'd say wouldn't make a lick of sense.
So even though I'd love to let go,
spread my wings,
let the flood gates open,
and let the subconscious take over,
revision is once again my superhero,
swooping down from the sky
as my hand slips from the ledge.

My Shine

They say that passing
through problems of life
brings out the shine.
If that's the case, then why,
as I'm passing through yet another problem
can I not see the shine in me?
I know I'm pushing it
and should give it more time,
but shouldn't there be a hint of shine by now,
a soft glow on the tip of my tongue
or a spark or two under my cheeks?
Am I not like everyone else?
Do I not have needs?
Maybe I'm looking too hard;
maybe it's only for others to see.
Whatever the reason,
there's still enough time to do the right thing.

The New Year

My journey here is ending,
but love is here,
has always been here
holding and keeping me safe.

When I close my eyes
things will not be the same,
but I'm ready
and though still afraid,
not nearly as afraid as before.

It's time to let go
and enter the life I was meant for,
the life I now love more than ever.

Andrew W. Lankford
Lollipops

Evening Prayer

Please help me
close my eyes
and get some rest
so I can wake refreshed
and ready to serve.
Please help me
think of good things
and not worry so much
about things out
of my control.
Thank You
for directing my steps,
for keeping me away from danger,
for bringing me back
to where I need to be.
Please hold me,
keep me close,
and never let me go.

~ The End ~

Andrew W. Lankford
Lollipops

Acknowledgments

I would like to thank the editors of the following journals in which the following poems, some in earlier versions, have appeared:

"A Beautiful Song" - *The Cypress Times*

"Blowing on a Fly" - *Hospital Drive: The University of Virginia*

"Lollipops" - *34th Parallel*

"Homework" - *Epiphany Online Magazine*

"On the Porch" - *Front Row Lit*

"Being Seen" -*Front Row Lit*

"The New Year" -*Living With Loss*

Thanks also to Marie McGaha and the world-class staff at *Dancing With Bear Publishing;* a bright future awaits. Finally, this collection would not have been possible without my friends and family around the world, especially my wife and best friend Sara, whose gentle patience and encouragement still mystify me.

Andrew W. Lankford
Lollipops

Andrew W. Lankford
Lollipops

Andrew W. Lankford
Lollipops

www.ingramcontent.com/pod-product-compliance
Lightning Source LLC
Chambersburg PA
CBHW060652030426
42337CB00017B/2575